For Susan—
Who never met a bear
She didn't love.
Here are more bear hugs
Back at ya!

Enjoy—

Love,
Melinda
Xmas '05

W9-BPK-363

BEAR HUGS

FOR

_____

FROM

_____

May the joy of
Christmas be with you
all year long!

FOR
YOU

BEAR HUGS FOR YOU AT CHRISTMAS

Copyright 2002 by Zondervan
ISBN 0-310-80154-0

Requests for information should be addressed to:

Inspirio, The gift group of Zondervan
Grand Rapids, Michigan 49530
http://www.inspiriogifts.com

Project Manager: Patti Matthews
Associate Editor: Jan Jacobson
Compiler and writer: Heidi Carvella
Contributor: Michael Vander Klipp
Design: Mark Veldheer
Photography: Synergy Photographic

Printed in China
02 03 04/HK/4 3 2 1

BEAR HUGS

FOR YOU AT CHRISTMAS

After Jesus was born in Bethlehem Magi from the east came to Jerusalem and asked, "Where is the one who has been born king of the Jews? We saw his star in the east and have come to worship him."

Matthew 2:1-2

Christmas is coming,
the geese are getting fat,
Please to put a penny in
the old man's hat;
If you haven't got a penny,
a ha'penny will do,
If you haven't got a ha'penny,
God bless you!

Beggar's rhyme

Who should ever stand
under the humble mistletoe,
no harm should befall them,
only a kiss, a token of love.

May you have the
gladness of Christmas
which is hope;
The spirit of Christmas
which is peace;
The heart of Christmas
which is love.

Ada V. Hendricks

Christmas!
The very word
brings joy to
our hearts.

Joan Winmill Brown

I heard the bells on
Christmas Day
Their old familiar
carols play,
And wild and sweet
the words repeat
Of peace on Earth,
good will to men!

Henry Wadsworth Longfellow

At Christmas
play and make
good cheer,

For Christmas
comes but
once a year.

Thomas Tusser

Let It Snow! Let It Snow! Let It Snow!

Sammy Cahn

May you have the
greatest two gifts of all
on these holidays;
someone to love and
someone who loves you.

John Sinor

Christmastime isn't the same if "snowbody" gets you with a snowball!

A hot mug
of cocoa with
plenty of fluffy
marshmallows
is a sweet,
warm hug
that comes from
the inside out.

Suddenly there was with the angel a multitude of the heavenly host praising God, and saying, "Glory to God in the highest, and on earth peace, good will toward men."

Luke 2:13-14 (KJV)

The gift of
genuine friendship
is more precious
than any packages.
True friendship is
a present that
gives generously
all year long.

Every good and perfect gift is from above.

James 1:17

Special friends
are the sweet
surprises in the
cookie dough of life!

Two are better than one, because they have a good return for their work.

Ecclesiastes 4:9

Have yourself a berry
little Christmas!

For unto us a child is born, unto us a son is given: and the government shall be upon his shoulder: and his name shall be called Wonderful, Counselor, The mighty God, The everlasting Father, The Prince of Peace.

Isaiah 9:6 (KJV)

Oh holy night!
The stars are brightly shining
It is the night of the dear Savior's birth!

Chappeau de Roquemaure

I'm dreaming of
a white Christmas,
Just like the ones
I used to know,
Where the tree
tops glisten
And children listen
To hear sleigh
bells in the snow.

Irving Berlin

Sending warm wishes
of love and blessings at
Christmas and always!

Your love has given me great joy and encouragement.

1 Philemon 1:7

Give thanks to the LORD,
for he is good;
his love endures forever.

1 Chronicles 16:34

The angel said to the shepherds, "Do not be afraid. I bring you good news of great joy that will be for all the people. Today in the town of David a Savior has been born to you; he is Christ the Lord."

Luke 2: 10-11

You will go out in joy
and be led forth in peace;
the mountains and hills
will burst into song before you,
and all the trees of the field
will clap their hands.

Isaiah 55:12

Shopping with a friend
not only makes the
crowds more bear–able,
it turns the whole
experience into
a celebration!

Let your light shine before men, that they may see your good deeds and praise your Father in heaven.

Matthew 5:16

I will honor Christmas
in my heart, and try
to keep it all the year.

Charles Dickens, as spoken by
Ebenezer Scrooge in A Christmas Carol

May the God of
hope fill you with
all joy and peace
as you trust in him.

Romans 15:13

The best gift you can give
at Christmas is yourself!

Joy to the world!

At least once a year, give in to the urge to lay down in the snow and make an angel!

C is for the Christ child born
   upon this day
H for Herald Angels in the night
R for our Redeemer
I for Israel
S for the star that shone so bright
T is for three wise men, they
   who traveled far
M is for the manger where he lay
A is for all he stands for
S means shepherds came
   And that's why there's a
   Christmas Day!

Deck the halls with boughs of holly,

Fa la la la la la la la la

'Tis the season to be jolly,

Fa la la la la la la la la!

A
Christmas
hug warms
the heart
and soul.

Be sure to count your blessings,
at Christmastime and always.

Happy Christmas to all,

and to all a good night!

Even if the holidays don't seem to go as planned, true love and friendship always shine through.

While they were in Bethlehem, the time came for the baby to be born, and she gave birth to her firstborn, a son. She wrapped him in cloths and placed him in a manger.

Luke 2:6-7